SMALL ARMS
OF THE
VIETNAM WAR

A PHOTOGRAPHIC STUDY

WARRIORS PUBLISHING GROUP
NORTH HILLS, CALIFORNIA

SMALL ARMS
OF THE
VIETNAM WAR

A PHOTOGRAPHIC STUDY

DALE A. DYE
and
TOM LAEMLEIN

SMALL ARMS OF THE VIETNAM WAR:
A PHOTOGRAPHIC STUDY

A Warriors Publishing Group book published by arrangement with the authors

PRINTING HISTORY

Warriors Publishing Group edition/August 2015. All rights reserved.

COPYRIGHT © 2015

by Dale A. Dye and Tom Laemlein
Cover art copyright © 2015 by Gerry Kissell gerrykissell.com

RIGHTS

ISBN 978-0-9861955-1-8
Library of Congress Control Number 2015908180

IMAGE CREDITS

Unless otherwise noted, the images in this book come from the United
States National Archives, the Patton Museum, and the photo collection
of the United States Marine Corps Historical Division. Others are in the
public domain because it is a work prepared by an officer or employee
of the U.S. Government as part of that person's official duties.

TABLE OF CONTENTS

INTRODUCTION
BY CAPT. DALE A. DYE, USMC (RET.)

Ask any veteran and you'll quickly discover there is nothing small about the small arms they carried into combat during the ten long years during which America and a few loyal allies fought a stubborn and determined enemy in Vietnam. To hear them tell it—and many more are willing to do so 40 years after the war ended—the weapons they carried or manned were the largest things in their lives. Despite the blanket military classification of their personal weapons as "small arms," the pistols, rifles, carbines, and machineguns used in action against elusive Viet Cong guerillas or conventional North Vietnamese Army units were keys to survival and success. Those who have fired individual or crew-served weapons at an enemy and suffered return fire in exchange for their efforts will always have indelible memories—fond or otherwise—of the small arms they carried in combat.

Anyone involved in ground combat bets his or her life on the weapons they carry for offensive or defensive action against an enemy carrying and relying on similar weapons. That's the nature of the beast in war. Army and Marine Corps infantrymen in Vietnam—and to a lesser but still crucial degree tankers, artillerymen and combat support troops—understood that from the moment they embarked on that first patrol in the jungle or dug in to defend a hard-won piece of misty high-ground. After a while, they became so comfortable with their weapons that they were more than a little antsy when those weapons were anywhere out of quick reach.

There is a very personal relationship that develops between a combat soldier or Marine and the weapon on which he relies for survival. It's an odd sort of love affair that has roots in practical application and in dogma such as the Rifleman's Creed (applicable to any personal firearm carried in combat) that says in part: *My rifle is human, even as I, because it is my life. Thus, I will learn it as a brother. I will learn its weaknesses, its strength, its parts, its accessories, its sights and its barrel. I will keep my rifle clean and ready, even as I am clean and ready. We will become part of each other.*

Infantry weapons continue to be crucial to more modern military forces engaged in worldwide combat zones that have kept them in action for even longer at this point than the American commitment to war in Vietnam. That's likely one of the reasons for an abiding interest in military small arms and certainly one the main drivers in putting together this book which provides not only some narrative concerning the details of the weapons of the Vietnam War but includes a large selection of rare photos that show those weapons and the men who carried them in action. To present this narrative and these pictures in palatable bites that can be easily consumed, we have organized this book in sections that cover particular types of weapons from pistols to heavy machineguns with some tangential coverage of things like grenade launchers and flamethrowers. And, of course, the enemy gets a vote here just as he does in combat, so we've included an overview of VC and NVA weapons at the end of the allied coverage.

It's our hope in this 40th anniversary year marking the troublesome end of the Vietnam War in 1975, that we've provided a study of interest to veterans both young and old who understand the crucial importance of small arms in warfare. In the midst of much technological innovation bordering on what would have been considered science fiction in the dark days of Vietnam, those people understand that nothing wins wars if it does not include that muddy, grimy, dog-tired infantryman with just his personal weapon to help him survive in a life and death encounter.

Pistols and revolvers are small, light, easy to conceal, fast to bring to bear, and may have more safety features than other firearms. Generally being an emergency self-defense weapon for use under 25 meters, a handgun bullet has neither the energy nor the accuracy of a bullet shot from a rifle.

1

PISTOLS AND REVOLVERS

PISTOLS AND REVOLVERS

The Colt M1911 .45 caliber pistol was in continuous service since its inception, seeing service in two world wars, Korea, Vietnam, and more.

As modern military forces worldwide developed and fielded reliable and accurate infantry shoulder weapons, pistols and revolvers became secondary weapons. The combat handgun was relegated in most nations to the role of self-defense weapon for officers not otherwise armed, a last-ditch back-up for gunners manning crew-served weapons, or as a survival tool for aircraft and combat vehicle crews. For the allied forces that fought in Vietnam, the two most common examples were the M1911A1 .45 caliber semi-auto issued to U.S. and ARVN forces and the Smith & Wesson Military & Police Model .38 caliber revolver carried by combat aircrews.

Given the close-quarters nature of most infantry combat engagements in Vietnam and some other special circumstances, the pistol took on a more important role than it was designed to fill. Notably, the venerable .45 pistol became the principal tool of "Tunnel Rats" who crawled into enemy bunkers, underground fortifications, and tunnel complexes generally armed with nothing more than a pistol and a flashlight. Combat narratives from veterans who engaged Viet Cong or North Vietnamese Army units at close ranges during the war are filled with stories of pistols used effectively when rifles or other weapons failed or fell short of ammunition. In such desperate engagements, the stopping power of the .45 ACP round was particularly praised as a rapid and reliable fight-ender.

Throughout the long war in Vietnam—and particularly in the early years when regulations regarding personal defense weapons were more lax—there is evidence that quite a number of combat soldiers and Marines carried civilian weapons either brought from home or sent by anxious family or friends. There was a particular up-tick in the appearance of civilian pistols and revolvers during the force-wide fielding of the M16 rifle when reports of regular battlefield malfunctions became widespread.

A 1st Infantry Division soldier operating near Bien Hoa uses what is likely a privately owned, short-barrel revolver in clearing an enemy position. While civilian style pistols and revolvers were strictly non-regulation, many found their way to Vietnam battlefields.

A helicopter crewman from the 1st Cavalry Division (Airmobile) bearing an issue .38 Caliber S&W revolver confers with fellow Army aviators near An Khe.

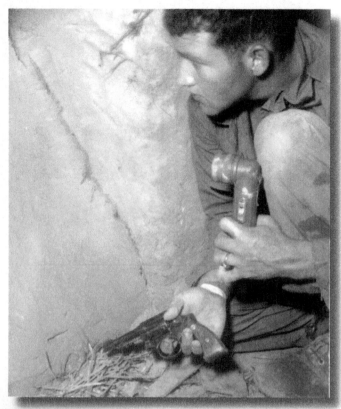

A 25th Infantry Division Tunnel Rat armed with an issue .38 caliber revolver checks an enemy trench line during Operation Cedar Falls in 1967.

A U.S. Army officer assigned as an adviser to ARVN units in the early years of the war carries a standard M1911A1 .45 caliber pistol in an issue shoulder-holster rig.

A Leatherneck with the 3rd Marine Division at Khe Sanh test fires his issue M1911A1 .45 along the perimeter of the infamous position prior to the start of the 1968 siege.

A 9th Infantry Division officer test fires his issue M1911A1 pistol on a range near Bear Cat.

A trooper from the 1st Cavalry Division keeps his his issue
M1911A1 .45 ready while escorting three VC suspects off the front
lines during Operation Thayer northeast of Saigon.

A Marine communicator keeps his issue .45 pistol ready during
a search and clear operation south of Danang.

During Operation Cedar
Falls, a soldier prepares
to enter an enemy tunnel
armed only with a flashlight
and his M1911A1 .45 pistol.

The Smith & Wesson Military and Police Model .38 caliber revolver like this one was standard issue for Air Force Security Police in Vietnam.

Leading his unit into an assault on enemy positions near Cam Lo, a Marine officer points the way with his M1911A1 pistol.

A Tunnel Rat from the 25th Infantry Division prepares to follow his .45 pistol into an underground enemy position during Operation Cedar Falls in the Hobo Woods.

Finished clearing an enemy tunnel during Operation Pershing, a 1st Cavalry Division trooper reaches for a helping hand while keeping his .45 pistol and flashlight at the ready.

A soldier of the 8th Infantry prepares to check an enemy position armed only with his issue .45 pistol while a fellow infantryman provides surface security.

Worming his way through an enemy tunnel, a 25th Infantry Division Tunnel Rat keeps his M1911A1 pistol ready for action.

A team of 1st Cavalry Division troopers prepares to investigate a captured enemy position during Operation Pershing. While his buddies take a closer look, the cover man has his .45 pistol ready for instant engagement.

A shoulder-fired automatic
firearm designed to fire
pistol cartridges from a
box magazine, combining
the automatic fire of
larger machineguns with
the portability and smaller
cartridge of a pistol.

2

SUBMACHINE GUNS

SUBMACHINE GUNS

The term submachine gun was coined by John T. Thompson, the inventor of the Thompson.

After World War II, the U.S. military had essentially given up on the concept of submachine guns. Even so, several types remained in the inventory of the American arsenal. By the time of the Vietnam War, the .45 caliber M3/M3A1 "Grease Gun" had been mostly withdrawn from front-line service but still equipped U.S. Army mechanized units and were part of the inventory of USMC special troops. The Grease Gun was supplied to ARVN troops, South Vietnamese Popular Forces, and also to the Montagnard mountain peoples. Rugged but rather slow firing—less than 500 rounds per minute—the Grease Gun was commonly found throughout the Vietnam War.

Large numbers of .45 caliber Thompson Submachine Guns, both the M1 and the M1A1 variant, were still kept in America's reserve stocks and many were supplied to ARVN troops and Vietnamese Popular Forces during the early 1960s. One of the finest submachine guns ever built, the Thompson was commonly seen in the early years of the Vietnam War—some had originally been brought to Vietnam by French forces in the 1950s, and some trickled down from China in the hands of Viet Cong troops. Some Thompson Gun copies were also fabricated in Vietnamese cottage workshops. The weight of the Thompson—more than 10.5 pounds unloaded—proved problematic for the slight build of the Vietnamese. Several photos show Vietnamese troops carrying the Thompson Gun with its buttstock removed.

Australian troops deployed to Vietnam with a small number of the 9mm Owen Submachine Gun. The World War II vintage Owen was a popular gun with the troops from down under and remained in Australian service until the mid-1960s.

Marines during a field recon exercise. The
man at left holds a M3A1 Grease Gun SMG.

Men of the 1st Australian Task Force at
Nui Dat during 1970. The man in the
foreground holds a M3 Grease Gun SMG.

Montagnards armed with M3A1
Grease Gun SMGs, March 1963.

A South Korean Marine holds a mud-splattered M3 Grease Gun during Operation Jefferson, February 1966.

SEALs during a stateside
training exercise. The lead
man carries a M3A1 SMG.

Above: A US advisor training Montagnards on the use of the
M3 Grease Gun submachine gun. February 1963.

Below: A Marine armed with an M3A1 SMG on patrol near Binh Thai during April 1965.

Above: Learning to use the Thompson gun: a US advisor instructs an ARVN Ranger on the finer points of shooting the M1A1 Thompson SMG during October, 1962.

Below: ARVN Rangers receive instruction on the Thompson SMG from a US Advisor during 1962.

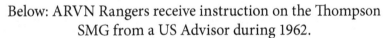

An ARVN soldier cleaning his Thompson SMG during 1963.

South Vietnamese girls equipped with the rare French MAS-38 submachine gun, a pre-WWII French design, chambered in the odd 7.65mm Longue. A very rare SMG even in Western Europe—they stopped making them around 1946.

An ARVN commander tours the battlefield during 1965. Note that one of his beret-wearing bodyguards carries a German-made WWII-vintage MP40 submachine gun. The other bodyguard carries an M16 rifle.

In the aftermath of the Tet Offensive: a US
ambassador tours the grounds of the US
embassy in Saigon while guarded by several State
Department Foreign Service officers, including
one armed with a Beretta Model 12 S (9mm).

ARVN troops interrogate a Viet Cong suspect during 1962. Note that both of the men carrying Thompson M1A1 SMGs have removed the buttstock of the weapon to reduce its weight. This practice would severely inhibit accurate shooting of the Thompson.

A US Navy man guards suspected Viet Cong
guerrillas during 1967. His weapon is a well-
worn Thompson M1A1 SMG, with two
30-round magazines wired together.

An ARVN soldier armed with a Thompson M1A1 submachine gun. Note the metal reinforcing band on the far end of the horizontal front hand-grip.

A rare look at a US Navy advisor ashore
during an early sweep in the Mekong Delta
area in 1964. He is armed with a Thompson
M1A1 SMG with the buttstock removed.

Above: An Australian radio operator stands by as a VC bunker
is detonated. He holds a 9mm Owen Submachine Gun.

Below: Supplied by the French with a mish-mash of weapons and equipment, this
ARVN soldier is seen on patrol in 1954 with a French-made MAT-49 (9mm) SMG.
This weapon was commonly found in Vietnam throughout the conflict and was also
re-chambered by the North Vietnamese to fire the 7.62x25mm Tokarev round.

A shotgun (also known as a scattergun or peppergun, or historically as a fowling piece) is a firearm that is usually designed to be fired from the shoulder, which uses the energy of a fixed shell to fire a number of small spherical pellets called shot, or a solid projectile called a slug.

3

SHOTGUNS

SHOTGUNS

When facing multiple opponents at close quarters, few weapons can match the shotgun. For urban combat, prisoner control, and shipboard operations it remains as deadly today as it was a century ago.

American military forces have carried shotguns in combat since World War I, when scatterguns proved particularly handy in brooming enemy forces out of linear trench lines where pinpoint accuracy and extended range was less important than simple blast effect. The consistent occurrence of close-range enemy ambushes in Vietnam brought the shotgun into regular front-line action from the mostly Military Police or prison-guard role it played in World War II and Korea. Shotguns—mainly eight-shot 12-gauge Remington Model 870 "riot-gun" types or variants—were issued in many infantry units as patrol weapons or for perimeter defense of firebases or other semi-permanent installations.

Soldiers or Marines armed with shotguns and walking point for combat patrols generally carried an alternating mix of 00 buckshot and slugs in their weapons. Virtually all shotgun rounds issued in Vietnam were either brass or plastic cased since the wet and humid jungle tended to be hard on cardboard casings. The issue shotgun loaded with double-ought buckshot could kill out to ranges of 30 meters and wound at double that distance. The major drawback was the spread of the nine balls contained in a buckshot round, making it possible to miss a man-size target at longer ranges, but an enemy engaged at five to ten meters was a sure kill for shotgunners. Marines, who carried a larger-than-usual number of 12-gauge shotguns into urban combat in Hue during Tet 1968, reported the weapon to be particularly effective in room-clearing engagements with NVA occupying houses or buildings in the embattled city.

During the mid-1960s when the war in Vietnam was in its bloodiest period, ordnance researchers were experimenting with "flechettes" for a variety of American weapons. Flechettes are best described as little—about 25mm—arrows, darts, or nails with fins. While flechette rounds were developed for a host of American weapons up to and including 105mm howitzers, most line infantrymen in Vietnam knew about them from using flechette rounds in shotguns. Both Remington and Winchester-Olin developed and fielded flechettes rounds for 12-gauge shotguns. These launched some 20 flechettes which were reportedly capable of penetrating flak-jackets and steel helmets out at ranges up to 400 meters, but most shotgunners found the flechette round most effective at 30 to 35 meters. The down-side of using flechettes in shotguns was a failure of the load to penetrate heavy jungle growth. An enemy behind a meter or two of bush was relatively safe from the effects of a flechettes round fired in his direction.

A Marine from the 3rd Marine Division operating near the DMZ humps with a Remington M10 shotgun for close work against enemy positions in the area. He has modified the issue sling with a field-expedient extension to make the weapon more handy.

Viet Cong weapons captured in the Mekong Delta included
a U.S. issue Remington M10 12-gauge riot gun.

ARVN troopers load up for a combat assault with a squad leader carrying
a Remington M31 12-gauge. Shotguns were not regular issue in ARVN
units but they showed up when required for specific missions.

Soldiers from the 127th Military Police Company patrol Qui Nhon Bay carrying weapons handy for boarding operations including a Remington M10 12-gauge shotgun rigged with barrel shroud and bayonet lug.

Dug into hasty defensive positions at Dak To, troopers from the 173rd Airborne Brigade stand ready for an enemy counterattack with individual weapons including a Remington M31 12-gauge shotgun.

Soldiers from the 716th MPs stand security watch outside the recently bombed Victoria Hotel in Saigon. One of the military policemen is armed with a Remington M31 12-gauge riot gun.

U.S. Navy SEALs prepare to disembark from an Army landing craft somewhere in the Mekong Delta. The SEAL on the left is armed with a Remington M31 12-gauge shotgun. SEALs operating in Vietnam generally carried weapons of their own choosing and the shotgun was a favorite for close-up ambush work.

A heavily loaded U.S. Marine radioman patrols near the DMZ armed with a Remington M10 12-gauge shotgun.

This American sailor, operating with the Navy's Junk Force in offshore waters, is armed with Savage M720 semi-automatic 12-gauge shotgun. Semi-autos found their way into American arsenals during the war but they were rare in infantry units.

A firearm, fired from
shoulder level, having a
long spirally grooved or
rifled barrel intended to
make a bullet spin and
thereby have greater
accuracy over a long
distance.

4

RIFLES AND CARBINES

RIFLES & CARBINES

The American-made M16 rifle was redesigned in 1966 to perform better in the wet, dirty conditions that prevailed in ground combat during the Vietnam War, and it became the weapon most commonly associated with U.S. troops in that conflict.

The vast majority of battlefield engagements in Vietnam involved soldiers exchanging fire from rifles of one form or another. The standard issue infantry shoulder-weapon early in the war was the M14 in 7.62mm carried by the Army and Marine units until that venerable weapons was replaced (sometimes forcibly as in the case of the U.S. Marine Corps resisting surrender of the longer-range and heavier-hitting rifle), by the M16 which was classified as an assault rifle owing to its selective-fire capability which allowed the rifleman an option of either semi-automatic or full-auto fire from a 20-round magazine of 5.56mm rounds. There were also bolt-guns carried primarily by trained snipers, and the venerable M1 Garand rifle saw plenty of service in the hands of many ARVN soldiers. By 1966 and throughout the remainder of the war, the M16A1—an improved version of the original—was the bog-standard infantryman's weapon of most allied forces in Vietnam. A notable exception was the 7.62mm L1A1 Self-loading Rifle (SLR) carried by Australian and New Zealander troops of the Royal Australian Regiment in Vietnam.

It's unreasonable to consider the M16—sometimes called the Matty Mattel rifle by critics of its plastic and steel construction and the black-rifle or widow-maker by fans of its light weight and firepower—without some attention to the teething problems of the initial-issue version of the weapon. Infantrymen were encountering excessive fouling of the rifle which resulted in jams and malfunctions at the worst possible times. A major Congressional investigation discovered there were essentially three major problems with the M16 and its issue ammo. These included a high-residue propellant which fouled the action after a magazine or two of fire, a lack of chromed chamber and barrel, and a lack of proper maintenance training and equipment among the troops carrying the weapon in jungle conditions. The Army quickly addressed these problems and came up with the M16Al—plus a blitzkrieg training program and the proper equipment for rifle maintenance—to produce one of the most significant and effective battle rifles of the 20th Century.

Carbines—lighter, shoulder-fired weapons with a shorter barrel than a rifle—are generally diminutive versions of full length weapons and designed to fire either the same ammo as a rifle or in most cases lower-powered rounds including those originally designed for military pistols. Familiar carbines such as the venerable U.S. M1 of World War II heritage and the M2, its select-fire variant, were often carried by ARVN regional forces and their American advisors early in the war. In a nod to ammo standardization and in an effort to improve the lethality of the standard carbine round, American ordnance designers in the mid-1960s fielded the CAR-15, essentially a carbine version of the M16 rifle with a collapsible stock assembly and made to fire the 5.56mm round from either 20 or 30 round magazines. These experimental weapons—official U.S. Army designation XM-177E1—began arriving in Vietnam in 1966 and met with approval by users who believed them to be the ideal weapon for commanders, radio operators, forward observers, dog handlers and others who needed more compact firepower. Despite glowing reports on the weapon, particularly from Special Operations troops, technical problems such as erratic rates of fire and consistent clogging due to residue after sustained automatic fire plagued the CAR-15 experiment. Production of the carbine was terminated in 1970 and soon thereafter it began to disappear from the battlefield as existing weapons were cannibalized for replacement parts.

CARBINES

An ARVN sailor serving with the Junk Force offshore in the South China Sea covers a suspect vessel with his M2 carbine. To make changes a bit quicker, he's taped another 30-round magazine to the one in his weapon.

The U.S. M1/M2 carbine showed up practically everywhere in Vietnam in both friendly and enemy hands. Captured carbines were a regular find among VC units. South Vietnamese forces loved the little carbine for its light weight and ease of handling. Early in the war most U.S. Advisors like the one shown here carrying a radio and conversing with a vilage boy in Long An Province, also carried the carbine to make ammo resupply easier.

A senior officer of the 173rd Airborne Brigade confers with a junior officer in the field during Operation Dayton in 1967. The officer on the right is carrying a carbine version of the standard M16 which was designated the XM-177.

This American Advisor to a South Vietnamese Popular Force unit is armed with the M2 selective fire version of the U.S. carbine which was issued with a 30-round magazine.

A 1st Air Cavalry Division trooper in the field near An Khe checks his XM-177 carbine version of the M16. The short carbine featured a collapsible stock, shorter barrel and several other minor modifications but it fired the standard 5.56mm round from standard 20-round magazines.

An officer from the 168th Engineer Battalion armed with an M2 carbine stands by the entrance to an enemy bunker that his team will shortly seal with explosives.

Squad member helps retrieve a 9th Infantry Divsion tunnel rat from an underground complex found near Dinh Tuong. The man on the left has his XM-177 carbine slung over his back to keep his hands free.

An ARVN paratrooper has supplemented the minimal firepower of his M1 carbine with a captured enemy RPD machinegun.

A unit of the 1st Air Cavalry Division waits for the helicopters that will lift them into combat. The NCO on the left is armed with an XM-177 carbine version of the standard M16 carried by the rest of the squad.

A Korean solider from the ROK Capitol Division stands watch at a firebase behind his M2 carbine.

A South Vietnamese Special Forces soldier returning from a long, deep patrol during which he was armed with the XM-177 carbine.

A pair of U.S. Advisors coach the CO of an ARVN unit operating near Saigon. The South Vietnamese soldiers are all armed with U.S. WW II weapons including the M1 carbine in foreground and the M1919 .30 caliber light machinegun carried by the ARVN soldier on the left.

A version of the XM-177 carbine equipped with a 4x scope which aided observation more than accurate shooting. The XM-177 was eventually standardized as the CAR-15 after relatively good experience with it in Vietnam.

An American sailor on duty at a small port facility on Vietnam's central coast, checks out a civilian vessel with his M2 carbine at hand.

M14

A Recon Marine, heavily armed for a long-range
patrol, checks his M14 prior to launch.

A Marine armed with an M14 guards an NVA prisoner
in early 1968. Some Marine Corps infantry units initially
resisted the mandated change from the M14 to the
M16 and kept stocks of the heavier rifle on hand.

A 1st Infantry Division squad leader directs his men while cradling an issue M14 with a pair of 20-round magazines taped together to give him extra ammo immediately at hand.

Early in the war, U.S. Army units like this platoon from the 1st Infantry Division carried the M14 into combat as the standard individual weapon.

A 1st Infantry Division NCO prepares to move his men, all armed with the M14 rifle, against an enemy position in mid-1965.

A Marine armed with an M14 pauses for a smoke while operating with his unit south of Danang in 1965.

Using an improvised extension for his issue sling, a Marine follows the muzzle of his M14 during a village sweep south of Danang.

With an Army combat cameraman filming their activities south of Saigon, a small unit of the 1st Infantry Division sets into a defensive position. The soldier being filmed is carrying the full-auto capable M14A1 with a pistol-grip stock.

A 1st Infantry Division soldier armed with an M14 rifle keeps watch for enemy movement from a position deep in a field of saw grass.

A 1st Infantry Division platoon calls for artillery
support while setting up a firing line of M14s
during operations south of Bien Hoa.

A 1st Infantry Division trooper keeps his M14A1 dry while negotiating a stream crossing in 1966. This weapon is a full-auto capable version of the M14 with pistol-grip stock and bipod legs.

During Operation Beacon Hill near the DMZ, a Marine humps out on patrol armed with an M14. Like many Marines who carried the rifle in combat, he has rigged an extension on the sling to make the weapon more handy in a hurry.

During Operation Utah in 1966, a left-handed 3rd Marine Division rifleman armed with an M14 fires on an enemy position.

While the official switch to M16s had been mandated for all combat units in Vietnam, the Marines kept the harder-hitting M14 at hand for quite some time. This rifleman uses one to blast away at NVA positions in Hue during Tet 1968.

A radioman from the 3rd Marine Division pauses with his
M14 to take a call during Operation Georgia in 1966.

1st Infantry Division soldiers armed with M14s
storm out of an M113 Armored Personnel Carrier
during an in-country training exercise.

A perimeter sentry from the 12th Aviation Battalion at Long
Binh sweeps the area for intruders over the sights of his M14.

A sentry from the 716th MP Battalion stands post near the Saigon River armed with an M14 rifle.

An ARVN Ranger operating on the outskirts of Saigon
during Tet 1968 rests a firm hand on his M14A1
rifle while his unit waits for word to move.

A shooter from the 26th Marines at Khe Sanh rests his M14 on sandbags while he aims in on enemy activity near the perimeter.

The scoped and accurized M14 was designated the M21 sniper rifle late in the war. It was fitted with a Leatherwood 3-9x Adjustable Ranging Scope and was the weapon of choice for 23rd Infantry Division soldiers undergoing in-country sniper training.

A sentry on duty overlooking the Phu Cuong Bridge mans his position armed with a scoped M14 for long-range observation and shooting.

During operations near Danang in 1965, a 3rd Marine Division rifleman rests his M14 on its bipod while waiitng for orders to advance.

M16

A camouflaged trooper with the 173rd Airborne Brigade operating in Vietnam sometime in 1965 keeps watch with his M16 rifle.

1st Cavalry Division troopers operating near Bong Son in 1966 take an enemy position under fire with their M16 rifles.

A trooper from the 101st Airborne Division takes a break in mid-1965 with his M16 at the ready.

A cannon crewman with the 19th Artillery supporting infantry operations during Operation Crazy Horse in 1966 keeps his M16 slung while he collects chow from a delivery to his firebase.

Troopers from the 1st Cavalry Division armed with issue M16's conduct a sweep through a village during Operation Irving in 1966.

A dog handler with the 25th Infantry Division waits to be called forward during a routine patrol in 1966. Most handlers carried the M16 ready to exploit any enemy alert from the scout dog.

Tropic Lightning troopers from the 25th ID sweep a
village near Cu Chi with M16s ready to engage.

Soldiers from the 1st Air Cavalry Division keep their M16s at the ready while searching a village northeast of Saigon.

In mid-1966, Soldiers from the 327th Infantry Regiment push forward with M16s blazing during Operation Hawthorne in Kontum Province.

A Screaming Eagle from the 101st Airborne pumps out automatic
fire from his M16 during Operation Cook in late 1967.

Helicopter crewmen such as this soldier from the 9th Infantry Division usually carried an M16 as a back-up weapon for ground action. This Huey crewman has neatly taped two 20-round magazines together to facilitate quick mag change in action. While many soldiers employed this field expedient, veterans did not recommend it as the bottom magazine with ammo exposed was subject to collecting dirt and debris.

A weary 9th Infantry Division soldier has found a piece of dry ground in the Mekong Delta but he's keeping his M16 loaded and close at hand.

These 9th Infantry Division soldiers operating in the Mekong Delta area of Vietnam had to be careful with their M16 rifles in the wet, muddy environment.

The muddy Mekong Delta area made it crucial for soldiers like this one from the 9th Infantry Division to constantly check and clean their M16 rifles.

An Army Special Forces trooper rests his M16 on early-issue bipod legs during a break in a long-range patrol. The leopard-skin camouflage was one several locally-manufactured patterns with which SF experimented early in the war years.

A Marine on field operations north of Danang keeps perimeter
watch with his M16 ready for instant engagement.

An assistant machinegunner with the 1st Infantry Division fires on enemy positions with his M16 somewhere in the Central Highlands.

A left-handed Marine engages enemy targets near Quang Tri in 1967. Left-handed shooters liked the M16 for ease of operation and vigorous ejectors that kept them from being showered with hot brass.

A pair of M16 armed grunts from the 5th Marine Regiment observe
an artillery strike over the sights of their rifles in 1967.

A Marine engaged in Operation Saline near the DMZ
opens up on an enemy shooter in late 1967.

A Marine from the 5th Regiment operating in the Arizona Territory pauses with a bayonet fixed on his M16. Marine units typically did not carry slings on their M16 rifles for a number of reasons including noise, a tendency to catch on brush in rough terrain and a belief that a rifle equipped with a sling will be on a shoulder when its needed in hand.

A 1st Marine Division Leatherneck advances on an enemy
position near Danang with his M16 spitting rounds.

During the fighting in Hue City, a rifleman with the 5th Marine Regiment
uses his M16 to cover the advance on an enemy-occupied building.

A Marine Interrogator-Translator Team interviews a captured NVA. Their M16s are resting at hand on early-issue bipod legs.

A U.S. Navy Hospital Corpsman escorts a wounded Marine out of the fighting. Typically, the Corpsman has retrieved the wounded man's weapon; in this case an M16 fitted with issue bipod legs.

A member of one of the Army's Long Range Reconnaissance Patrol (LRRP) units maneuvers cautiously through jungle terrain following the muzzle of his M16 rifle.

A 25th Infantry Division rifleman festooned with extra machinegun ammo crosses a rice paddy with his M16 ready for instant action.

South Vietnamese sailors patrolling Qui Nhon Harbor cover a boarding party with their M16 rifles.

An Army Special Forces soldier takes to the field wearing tiger stripe camouflage uniform and carrying an M16 that's been modified with a short-range telescopic sight. He's also dropped the hinged trigger guard for quicker access and taped a couple of 20-round magazines together to facilitate combat reloads.

A 101st Airborne Brigade soldier engages targets using an M16
fitted with an XM-148 experimental grenade launcher.

A solider with the 173rd Airborne Brigade pauses in the field with his
specially-equipped M16. The weapon carries an XM-148 40mm grenade
launcher slung below the barrel. This rifle-launcher combination was an early
attempt to improve on the M79 while giving grenadiers more firepower.

A SEAL operating in the murky Rung Sat Special Zone keeps
watch in the bow of a local boat with his M16 ready.

This photo provides a good look at the backpack carried by soldiers using the Army's experimental E-63 Personnel Detector, known to almost everyone as a "people sniffer."

Left: The sensor/collector device of the E-63 manpack people sniffer
was mounted near the muzzle of a standard M16 rifle.

Right: The E-63 personnel detector operator swept the bush like this trooper from
the 1st Cavalry Division, hoping the unit would detect human sweat or urine. The
People Sniffer just as often detected the presence of animals, friendly soldiers or
even its operator. The experiment was never very popular or successful.

Above: This fully-rigged and modified M16 rifle was issued to USAF Security
Police at Tan Son Nhut Airbase for perimeter patrols. It features an attached
AN/PVS-2 Starlight Scope and an XM-148 grenade launcher.

Below: A rifleman with the 26th Marines at Khe Sanh engages what
might be enemy infiltrators along the base airstrip.

A dramatic skyline view of a Marine sentry with his M16 on duty near a patrol base perimeter.

A 9th Infantry Division soldier operation near Bear Cat sweeps the terrain with an AN/PVS-2 Starlight Scope mounted to his M16 rifle. The scope, which essentially intensified ambient starlight in darkened conditions could be used weapon mounted or handheld.

An assistant guides his M60 gunner onto target. Many A-gunners carried a magazine of tracers for their M16s which could be used to mark targets.

During a rice-paddy sweep in early 1967, this soldier, carrying
an M16 with an XM-148 grenade launcher attached, is wearing
a Field Protective Mask for some unexplained reason.

An assistant machinegunner from 2nd Battalion, Royal Australian Regiment ready to move out with his L1A1 Self-Loading Rifle (SLR) loaded and locked. The FN FAL was fairly heavy for confined jungle work at nearly 10 pounds unloaded but the Aussies swore by its knock-down power in combat.

An infantry light section from 1st Battalion, RAR mans a firebase perimeter near Bien Hoa. While the riflemen are armed with the standard L1A1 rifle, their support is provided by a U.S. M60 machinegun.

Soldiers from the RAR arriving for duty in Vietnam. They are all armed with Australia's standard infantry rifle at the time, the L1A1 SLR.

Above: An Australian officer and his radioman pause to transmit on a jungle operation. The soldier carrying the radio backpack is armed with the Aussie standard L1A1 self-loading rifle.

Below: A good look at fairly standard Australian infantry field kit all built around the L1A1 SLR. The rifle in foreground has an Aussies battle dressing taped to the butt-stock.

Following a 1968 firefight near Bien Hoa, a squad of RAR troopers armed with L1A1 rifles prepares to sweep forward and assess the results.

A rifle platoon from the RAR engages the enemy dug in around Nui Thi Vai in 1968. The prone soldiers are firing cover for a maneuver element with their L1A1 rifles.

An ARVN trooper radios a report with his trusty M1 rifle nearby. The uniform and radio mark this as a photo taken very early in the war.

An ARVN Ranger unit in training practices river crossings via small inflatable boat. The shooters here are all armed with the M1 rifle which was heavy and long for the average ARVN soldier. Despite those concerns, ARVN units and local militia units made effective use of the Garand in combat.

An ARVN Ranger patrol prepares to cross a water obstacle by securing their M1 rifles to plastic-wrapped equipment bundles.

Above: An ARVN crew from the 11th Armored Cavalry Regiment lines up to draw water and rations from their U.S. counterparts. The South Vietnamese soldiers are all armed with the M1 Garand rifle.

Below: Two ARVN officer candidates in training stand watch in a bivouac armed with the M1 Garand rifle.

A U.S. Army Ranger Advisor demonstrates proper assault fire position with the M1 rifle for a class in the field near Saigon.

A Marine armorer at Camp Pendleton, CA checks a Remington Model 700 sniper rifle due for shipment to Vietnam.

During the early years of the war, Marine snipers like this one operating with the 3rd Marine Division on Operation Harvest Moon, used a number of experimental scopes on the 7.62mm Remington Model 700s including the Unertel shown here.

A Marine Corps sniper team in over-watch position covers infantry maneuvers to their front. This Remington heavy-barrel rifle carries an ART (Adjustable Ranging Telescope) sight which, along with several other modifications of the Model 700, composed what the Corps called the M40 sniper weapon system.

Above: A Marine sniper and his spotter operating with 3rd Battalion, 7th Marines in Vietnam scans for targets with his Remington Model 700 rifle resting on his helmet for additional stability.

Below: A Marine sniper using an M40 rifle and scope combination aims in on a target being pointed out by his spotter.

A 1st Marine Division sniper team scans enemy territory for targets
using the rifle's telescopic sight and a standard spotting scope.

A general purpose
machinegun is designed
to be employed by an
individual soldier, with or
without an assistant, as an
infantry support weapon.
It generally has a caliber
no greater than .30 inch or
7.62mm.

5

GENERAL PURPOSE
MACHINEGUNS

GENERAL PURPOSE MACHINEGUNS

General Purpose or Light Machineguns are designed to be carried by infantry. Most are fired from a bipod or light tripod but can be fired from the hip in an emergency.

Second only to the rifle on Vietnam battlefields, the General Purpose or Light Machinegun (LMG) was the most common direct-fire weapon used by infantrymen in battle with units of the Viet Cong and North Vietnamese Army. Allied small-unit offensive tactics were designed and employed around a base of fire provided by machinegun crews, who pounded targets and covered riflemen maneuvering against enemy formations or fortifications. In the defense of hard-won positions, strategic firebases, or other installations, the LMG was always positioned in pivotal locations to sweep enemy attackers with rapid, well-aimed fire.

There were generally two basic models of LMG employed by allied forces facing the Viet Cong and NVA. A very common LMG, particularly among line ARVN infantry, Popular Force and Regional Force units was the M1919A4 Browning, which was issued as a crew-served weapon with tripod, T&E device, and other accoutrements. Those Americans who operated in proximity to ARVN units often saw the .30 caliber weapon in its A6 variant which included a carrying handle, shoulder stock, and bipod. The M1919A4 also saw extensive service in American units primarily as a coaxial weapon on tanks or an infantry-support weapon on Armored Personnel Carriers (APCs) and wheeled vehicles of several types. While it couldn't be called the workhorse GPMG in Vietnam, the venerable Browning air-cooled .30 caliber showed up in some very interesting and diverse places throughout the war.

The most common crew-served infantry support weapon on Vietnam battlefields was the M60 GPMG, affectionately known as The Pig due to its 28-pound unloaded weight. The M60, manned by a trained gunner and his assistant, fired the 7.62mm round from belts of 200 strung together in disintegrating metal links at the rapid rate of 800 rounds per minute. It was a reliable, hard-hitting weapon with an action modeled on the German MG-42 system. It had a rugged bipod that was standard infantry issue, but could also—although rarely in the field—be fired from an issue tripod that included a precision-fire traversing and elevating device. The weapon had an interchangeable barrel that was supposed to be switched out periodically with a spare carried by the assistant machinegunner, although in practice these spare barrels often disappeared or were disregarded in the heat of combat. Trained and talented M60 gunners kept the barrels relatively cool by firing in constrained bursts of eight to ten rounds. During sustained fire, it was common for gunners to cool the barrels with Lubricant Small Arms (LSA) although the practice engendered clouds of steam marking the gun's position. While the M60 GPMG gained well-deserved fame in the small-unit infantry support role, it was also fitted via pedestal or traversing ring-mounts on vehicles such as APCs, trucks, and Jeeps. One of the most familiar and effective uses of the M60 GPMG was the primary weapon of otherwise unarmed helicopters in Vietnam. Initially hung from bungee cords in the doors of various helicopters and later on specially designed pedestal mounts, the M60 GPMG was very effective as a suppression or defensive weapon in the hands of skilled door-gunners.

Firing downhill from a completely unconventional position, a Marine machinegunner hammers a jungle target with his M60 LMG.

Ordnance men from one of the Navy helicopter squadrons operating in Vietnam rigged a pair of M1919A4 .30 calibers in a dual-mount to give their door gunner a more lethal punch.

A small unit of shore-based South Vietnamese sailors mans a tripod-mounted Browning .30 caliber LMG to defend their port facilities.

A Marine infantryman prepares to mount an LVTP-5 amphibian tractor somewhere in the South China Sea. He's carrying one of the M1919A4 .30 calibers that the armor crews typically used to protect the vehicle.

Following an enemy sapper attack on the flight-line at Tan Son Nhut
airbase near Saigon, an Air Force security detachment surveys the damage
from an M151 Jeep bearing a pintle-mounted M60 machinegun.

The disintegrating-link ammunition belt that fed the M60 LMG in action had a tendency to kink when gravity worked against the action so gunners quickly came up with a field-expedient solution that involved wiring a C-ration can to the feed ramp which gave the ammo belt an easier path into the gun.

A Marine manning a bunker near the Danang Air Base checks his M-60 which has been stabilized on a layer of sandbags. This view gives a good look at the LMG with all the issue bells and whistles including the traversing and elevating device on the tripod.

Some Army aviation units flying Huey's with M60D models
fixed as door guns were also issued a metallic feed chute
which kept belted ammunition from flopping around when
the aircraft was maneuvering at high speed. This modification
greatly reduced jams and was popular with door gunners.

A Huey door gunner flying in an aircraft from the 175th Aviation Company in Vietnam provides a good look at the M60D configuration LMG which featured a ring sight, spade hand-grips and no fore end. This model of the M60 became standard on all Army helicopters by the mid-point of the war years.

A Marine M60 gunner in a fixed hilltop position near Khe Sanh used logs to improve support for his weapon and keeps field glasses close at hand to spot enemy movement.

A 1st Infantry Division M60 machinegun team sprints across open ground during an operation in mid-1968. The assistant gunner is struggling to keep a long belt of linked ammo out of the dirt and connected to the gun.

An M60 gunner from the 5th Marines opens up on an enemy position firing his M60 from an unsupported position. While firing a rifle from a kneeling or off-hand (standing) position was a relatively simple proposition, controlling the LMG without support from bipods or a tripod took a strong man with plenty of experience.

An Army M60 gunner wrapped with spare ammo belts takes break in the jungle. While some units objected to the Mexican bandito method of carrying spare LMG ammo claiming it was damaged or lost in rough terrain, almost all machinegun crews in Vietnam carried their spare round this way at some time if not always.

Soldiers from the 18th MP Brigade jury-rigged a Jeep with add-on armor and then mounted an M60 on the roof for fire support.

An M60 gunner from the 5th Marines uses a bullet-pocked palm tree to help steady his weapon during the fighting in Hue City.

Vietnamese Popular Forces train with the M60 under the watchful eye of an American advisor.

Engaging targets with the M60 from an off-hand or standing position took a strong man with plenty of experience behind the gun.

A Marine machinegun crew sweeps a disputed treeline with M60 fire. The Assistant Gunner did more than carry extra ammo and keep the gun loaded. He could adjust the gunner's strike on selected targets by a series of practiced touches or kicks.

The M60 LMG did service with American forces on any
number of wheeled and tracked vehicles like this M42 Duster,
a self-propelled 40mm anti-aircraft weapon system that was
pressed into infantry fire-support duty in Vietnam.

Marines defending the Khe Sanh perimeter have mounted their M60 LMG
on its issue tripod. The tripod was rarely carried on patrol in the bush
where machinegun crews made do with the M60's folding bipods.

Soldiers defending the perimeter of a mountain firebase in
early 1970 sweep the ground below with an M60 LMG.

Veteran grunt machinegunners like this one from the 1st Marine
Division found the cross-shoulder method of carry most comfortable
for humping the M60 until contact was imminent.

This Recon Marine machinegunner patrolling north of Con Thien has fixed
a rifle sling on his M60 to make carry and assault fire a little easier.

This familiar image of an M60 machinegunner from the 173rd Airborne Brigade demonstrates the amount of extra ammo a grunt platoon was willing to carry to keep the machinegun in action.

This M60 mount is typical of those used to support M60 LMGs as defensive weapons on transport helicopters in Vietnam. Typically there were two M60s mounted in helicopters like this CH-46 Sea Knight flying in support of Marines patrolling south of Danang.

An M60A1 gunner from the 3rd Marine Division operating near the DMZ conducts reconnaissance by fire on a suspect treeline in 1967.

Crewmen manning an O-1 Bird Dog have found a way of fitting an aviation configured M60 LMG as a defensive weapon on their light observation aircraft.

Early in the war before special mounts and gun configurations were available, door gunners like this one aboard a Huey gunship of the 179th Aviation Company jury-rigged their ground version M60s to hang from bungee-cords.

This Army machinegunner with his M60 somewhere in III Corps during 1970 has draped himself with all the spare ammo he can carry. Some units discouraged this method of carrying spare machinegun ammo over concern for loss or damage to the belts, but gun teams usually ignored it.

The U.S. military defines "assault rifles" as short, compact, selective-fire weapons that employ a cartridge intermediate in power between submachine gun and rifle cartridges. That would include the M16 and the AK-47, but there were some outliers—weapons with arguable classification—that saw limited service in Vietnam.

BARs and the Stoner System

BARs AND THE STONER SYSTEM

For nearly 50 years, the BAR reigned supreme on the battlefield.

Most ordnance technical experts and gun gurus can agree that a true "assault rifle" is an individual, selective-fire weapon that feeds an intermediate cartridge from a detachable magazine. That's about all they can agree on when it comes to classifying the plethora of weapon types that wound up being used in the long war in Vietnam. For instance, there are those who insist that the venerable American M1918 Browning Automatic Rifle should really be classified as a light machinegun. And there are those who argue that the Stoner weapon system, employed by Navy SEAL teams and tested by the U.S. Marines in Vietnam, is both light machinegun and assault rifle depending on configuration. These disputes mark those weapons as outliers in our book.

In Vietnam, the BAR, most commonly encountered in the hands of ARVN troops, was most often used as a base of fire covering maneuver elements in combat or as a strongpoint in static defensive positions. Since the BAR fired the same .30 caliber standard ammo as the M-1 Garand rifle and the M1919 series of machineguns with which they were typically equipped for most of the war years, commonality of ammunition was a plus for South Vietnamese units. At a hefty 19 pounds and 48 inches long, the BAR was a handful for diminutive ARVN troops but they learned to use it with great skill and effectiveness, especially during the early years of the war. Some American units employed BARs during the war but these were mostly Navy or garrison units that still had older weapons in their inventories or had traded with the ARVN to supply themselves with a little more firepower. In the fight for Hue City during Tet 1968 when American Marines overran an abandoned ARVN armory, several BARs were purloined and put to good use against the NVA in subsequent street fighting. VC and NVA units were not above capturing and using the BAR wherever they could get their hands on it but ammo resupply was always a problem for them.

Weapons wizard Eugene Stoner designed the firearm system that bears his name in the early 1960s. He built the prototype and submitted it for purchase to the Department of Defense as the Stoner 63 in 1963. The American military quickly became interested as the war in

Vietnam was heating up and teething problems were being encountered with the newly introduced M16 rifle. The military adopted the system for experimental use and it was variously classified as the M63, XM-22, XM-23, XM-207 and the MK-23 Mod 0 in light machinegun configuration. The Stoner 63 system was truly flexible and could be readily configured and used as either an assault rifle or as a light machinegun. For practical purposes it was hard for users to tell the difference with the exception of how the weapon was employed tactically. The Stoner fired the same NATO standard 5.56mm round from either a drum magazine or a standard box magazine and was relatively handy in the bush at just under 12 pounds. The select-fire Stoner was listed as effective at ranges out to 800-plus meters and could put out some serious heat at rates of from 700-1,000 rounds per minute. U.S. Navy SEAL teams liked the Stoner and carried it on many deep operations almost until the end of the war. The Marines showed some early interest and issued Stoners to one rifle company (Lima Co., 3rd Battalion, 9th Marines) for testing in Vietnam. The weapon was given a lukewarm evaluation and the Marines decided against any further expenditure on the Stoner.

While a regular ARVN infantryman watches with his M1 carried like a
squirrel-hunter, a small unit of Popular Forces scrambles into a sampan
for a river crossing. The BAR carried by one of the PFs will be about
all the fire-support this unit can expect if they run into VC.

A soldier with the 199th Light Infantry Brigade keeps an M1918A1
Browning Automatic Rifle dry while crossing a deep water obstacle.
The BAR was not regularly issued to U.S. units in Vietnam but
the old, reliable fire support weapon often found its way back into
American hands, usually as a result of a swap with ARVN units.

A Navy Chief Petty Officer stands guard with a BAR while crews
load an Australian aircraft somewhere in IV Corps.

ARVN soldiers in training near Saigon in 1970 conduct familiarization
fire with the M1918A1 Browning Automatic Rifle.

Sailors aboard one of the U.S. Navy's Riverine support ships keep a close eye on the shoreline for enemy movment. They have added a BAR to their available firepower.

A couple of Marines explore the BAR they've acquired somewhere. The M1918A1 was regularly found in ARVN RF and PF forces. The argument continues among experts and pundits whether it should be classified as an assault rifle or a light machinegun. In the end it depends on how the weapon is used.

Returning from a productive local patrol, an ARVN Popular Forces soldier carries his muddy and well-used BAR over the shoulder. The weapon was initially issued with a sling but encountering one in use in Vietnam was rare.

A good view of a Navy SEAL in the Mekong Delta in an over watch position
with his Stoner 63 fitted with the optional 150-round drum magazine.

The Stoner system, officially classified as the MK 23 could be used as either
a standard assault weapon or a light machinegun,. Unlike the M-60 LMG,
the Stoner could be configured to feed from either side of the gun.

This is a rare look at the Stoner 63 assault rifle (M63A1) being used in Vietnam by members of Lima Company, 3rd Battalion, 9th Marines. The experimental Stoner system firing the same 5.56 x 45mm round as the M16, was only issued to some Navy SEALs and one company of Marines to see how it fared in jungle combat. The experiment yielded something less than sterling results and the Stoner was never approved for general issue.

This familiar photo shows a U.S. Navy SEAL on a mission early in
the war. He's got the standard drum magazine loaded on his Stoner
with several belts of extra ammo draped over his shoulders.

A tripod- or vehicle-
mounted weapon served
by a crew of three to
seven men and designed
to provide sustained fire
from a prepared position
or mobile platform.

7

HEAVY
MACHINEGUNS

HEAVY MACHINEGUNS

The M2HB was used in Korea and Vietnam, and later in both Operation Desert Storm, the Afghan theater of Operation Enduring Freedom, and in Iraq.

At nearly 130 pounds with its tripod, the venerable M2HB (Heavy Barrel) .50 caliber machineguns can hardly be classified as small arms but they played such a significant role in Vietnam that the long-range and heavy-hitting Ma Deuce deserves special consideration. Ground-mounted on the M3 tripod, fixed to armored vehicles or hammering away from various ring or pedestal mounts in virtually everything that could roll in Vietnam; the M2 was a favored weapon in both the offense and defense throughout the war in Southeast Asia.

To this day on battlefields around the world, the M2 .50 caliber HMG is proof positive of the maxim that says if it ain't broke, don't fix it. John Moses Browning's innovative design was initially adopted by the U.S. Army in the waning days of World War I as an antiaircraft weapon. It's been onward and upward since then. The heavy weapon—especially when fired from its tripod with a Traversing & Elevating (T&E) device—is extremely steady and stable, capable of accurately engaging targets out to 2,000 meters. Various Army and Marine units in Vietnam sometimes used the weapon in concert with ordnance optics as a long-range sniper weapon. There are also a number of instances on record where the M2 was fitted with Starlight scopes for effective nighttime engagements.

While it was too heavy for infantry units to carry with them on patrols in the bush, the M2 was often fixed as a fire-support weapon on high ground or on strategically sited vehicles to provide covering fire for maneuvering units. Firing from roof mounts on the trucks that regularly convoyed people and supplies to far-flung locations throughout Vietnam, .50 caliber machineguns firing heavy slugs at the rate of 550 rounds per minute were effective in disrupting enemy ambushes. As more and more helicopter types entered the fray in Vietnam, M2s were affixed to medium- and heavy-lift rotary-wing aircraft and were extremely handy for suppressing enemy action in contested landing zones.

A soldier from the 1st Cavalry Division mans a strongpoint along
Vietnamese Route 19 behind an M2 HB .50 caliber machinegun.

A crewman from the 53rd Aviation Detachment arranges ammo for an M2 rigged as a door gun aboard his CH-47 Chinook transport helicopter.

An artilleryman from the 12th Marines based near the DMZ cleans one of the M2 .50 caliber machineguns his battery uses for perimeter defense.

Engineers from the Army's 937th Engineer Group have used spare culvert material to fashion a gun-tub for this .50 caliber machinegun near Pleiku.

A trooper from the 173rd Airborne Brigade pumps fire onto a target near LZ English in 1969. This M2 is rigged to a pintle mount on an M151 Jeep.

A gunner with the 9th Infantry Division used an M2 .50 caliber
to pound a target in the Mekong Delta. This heavy machinegun
has been mounted on an M113 Armored Personnel Carrier.

A crew from the U.S. Army's 2nd Field Artillery Group rigs an
M45 quad .50 on the bed of a 2.5 ton truck to build the familiar
gun truck employed as convoy escorts all over Vietnam.

An Army crewman folds a belt of .50 caliber ammo into the feed bin of an M45 quad mount. The versatile mount for four M2 heavy machineguns could be employed as fixed ground position or fitted to any number of vehicles.

This M2 HB .50 caliber employed by the U.S. 9th Infantry Division in operations near Dong Tam has been fitted with a starlight scope for employment as a long-range weapon during night operations.

A quad .50 in a ground mount near a disputed LZ provides covering perimeter security for a battery from the 41st Artillery in 1968.

A good look at the business end of an M45 quad .50 mount on the perimeter of LZ Bastogne in 1970.

A well-sandbagged .50 caliber machinegun is the main defensive
armament aboard this barge being operated on an inland waterway
by the U.S. Army's 1099th Transportation Company in 1967.

A good look at a U.S. Army standard Armored Cavalry Assault Vehicle which was
basically an up-gunned version of the M113 APC. The .50 caliber mounted in an
armored gun-tub with protective shielding was the vehicle's heaviest weapon.

U.S. Navy gunboat crews operating on Vietnam's inland waterways employed a number of innovative weapon configurations like this mount that featured a standard M2 .50 caliber machinegun mounted atop an 81mm mortar tube.

Some variants of the U.S. Navy's Patrol Boat Riverine (PBR) featured .50 calibers as twin mounts in gun-tubs that were originally designed for anti-aircraft defense.

An interesting look at the heavy machineguns of the M45 quad mount from the crewman's perspective. The guns had to be specially configured to feed from opposite sides to maintain a reliable ammo flow.

A flotilla of U.S. Navy patrol boats carries an ARVN assault unit unit toward an objective in the Mekong Delta. The .50 caliber mounted atop an 81mm mortar will provide preparatory fire and support when the infantry is landed.

This American sailor aboard a fire support boat is manning a
gun position that is rigged with a .50 caliber machinegun plus
an experimental automatic 40mm grenade launcher.

The business end of the U.S. Navy's specially configured gun mount for
Riverine Patrol Boats shows the .50 caliber and the 81mm mortar mounted
below. The logo on the mortar's recoil tube translates loosely as "kill VC."

A Navy crewman aboard a shark-mouth painted PBR scans
the shoreline for enemy activity at his station near the
forward mounted M2 HB .50 caliber machinegun.

A good look at the triggers inside the spade-grips of a military standard
M2 heavy-barrel machinegun. A good gunner developed a touch
that let him easily fire single shots or short, controlled bursts.

The dual mount for twin .50 calibers aboard Navy fire support boats featured a specially-rigged set of remote triggers attached to the fixture for control of both guns as a unit.

The U.S. Army's convoy escort of fire support gun trucks were often locally rigged as missions required. This fairly common configuration features four .50 calibers in an M45 mount plus an M60 for added punch. Both gun positions have been rigged with what looks like headlamps, presumably for night operations.

Early in the war, a Marine tank crew has rigged a ground-mount .50 caliber with tripod atop their vehicle for additional fire support. The Marine standard M48A3 main battle tank had a .50 caliber mounted in a cupola atop the turret but the weapon suffered from frequent jams due to feeding problems.

A pair of U.S. Marine gunners adjust the headspace and timing on an
M2 HB .50 caliber machinegun in 1970 somewhere near the DMZ.

In the middle of a monsoon rain, a U.S. Marine crew mans an M45 quad
.50 caliber mount covering a patrol base in the Que Son Mountains.

A grenade launcher is a weapon that launches a specially designed grenade or a grenade cartridge with more accuracy, higher velocity, and to greater distances than a soldier could throw it by hand. A flamethrower is a mechanical incendiary device designed to project a long, controllable stream of fire.

GRENADE LAUNCHERS AND FLAMETHROWERS

GRENADE LAUNCHERS AND FLAMETHROWERS

The rifled grenade launcher was ideal for Vietnam. It was suited to most terrains and could multitask successfully because of the effective array of munitions.

American infantry units entered the war in Vietnam with designated grenadiers in rifle squads carrying the M79 grenade launcher with a bore diameter of 40mm. Known affectionately as the "blooper" for the sound it made when fired, the M79 was adopted by the U.S. Army in 1961to deliver a high-explosive round between the longest range of the hand grenade (30-40 meters) and the mid-range of the 60mm mortar (300-400 meters). It proved to be deadly efficient in the hands of a trained, field-experienced grenadier. ARVN regional local forces made due with older rifle grenade launchers fired from their vintage M1 rifles, but regular South Vietnamese Army and Marine units were quickly equipped with M79s making the weapon the most commonly encountered grenade launcher throughout the war.

The M79 basically resembled a single-shot, sawed-off shotgun and functioned much like that firearm, requiring the shooter to break open the weapon for loading and ejecting the fired projectile casing. There were a number of different rounds developed for the Blooper and fielded in Vietnam but the most common was the HE or high-explosive round that had a lethal bursting radius of five meters and produced wounds out to about 15 meters. The fuse in the standard 40mm HE round for the M79 did not arm until it had traveled 30 meters from the muzzle which presented problems when grenadiers encountered enemies at closer ranges. To address this situation, the Army developed and fielded both flechette and buckshot filled M79 rounds which launched their projectiles in plastic sabots. Both of these rounds were deadly in close encounters. There were also pyrotechnic and CS gas rounds fielded for use by M79 grenadiers in both Army and Marine Corps units in Vietnam.

By 1966, the U.S. Army began experimenting with a grenade launcher fixed to the M16 rifle that gave soldiers the ability to function as both grenadier and rifleman. The experimental version fielded in Vietnam in early 1967 was called the XM-148. It was tested by a number of line infantry units but there were consistent complaints about basic safety, reliability, and awkward battle sights. The experiment was terminated in May and Army grenadiers went back to the M79 while carrying a .45 pistol as their back-up weapon. An improved rifle-grenade launcher configuration—what would become today's M203—was briefly tested late in the war, but for the most part the standard grenade launcher carried by infantry units remained the M79 Blooper. There were also experiments in Vietnam with externally powered or hand-cranked automatic grenade launchers mounted on vehicles and Navy Riverine craft, but never more than a few hundred were ever used in combat.

Since flamethrowers had proved lethal against Japanese forces dug in on jungle islands in the Pacific during World War II, there was an initial thought that these weapons would be equally effective against Viet Cong forces in Vietnam who were notorious for using bunkers, caves, and tunnels as fighting positions. Army and Marine infantry units arriving in Vietnam were equipped with the Korean War era M2A1-7 or the more modern variant M9A1-7 man-portable, backpack flamethrowers, and both models were used in some combat operations, particularly against fortified positions or to burn out enemies hiding in countryside villages. Due to its weight—nearly 70 pounds with a full fuel load that had to be humped through steaming jungle terrain and intense heat—plus the difficulty in obtaining reloads from remote locations, the flamethrower never became a big player in Vietnam combat operations.

The most common flamethrower used by the Army and Marine Corps in Vietnam was the M9A1-7 model that had an effective range of about 65 feet and a firing duration of only 10-20 seconds before the four gallons of fuel contained in two tanks on the gunner's back were exhausted. For the most part, except for operations where transport was available and situations favored attack with flame weapons, the flamethrower in Vietnam did more service burning off undergrowth around fixed installations than it did in infantry combat.

Operating in the Iron Triangle area during Operation Cedar Falls, a soldier from the 1st Infantry Division prepares to burn out an enemy position with the issue standard M9-7 flamethrower. The weapon had a nominal range of 50 meters with thickened fuel but was often used at much closer ranges on bunkers and underground enemy positions.

A trooper with the 1st Air Cavalry division armed with an M79 grenade launcher pauses during Operation Irving to phone in a position report.

Troopers with the 173rd Airborne Brigade escort a flamethrower operator
up HIll 875 where the weapon will be used against enemy bunkers.

A Marine Corps flame team uses an M9-7 flamethrower to burn out
enemy structures. The weapon was heavy for jungle operations and
had a very limited firing time of only five to eight seconds but it was
useful in certain dedicated operations against fortified positions.

On a firing line near Bien Hoa, a trooper from the 101st Airborne Division practices long-range, high-angle fire with the M79 grenade launcher.

An ordnance officer demonstrates loading the CS gas round into the M79.

A Marine operator burns out a patch of enemy-occupied bush with the issue M9-7 flamethrower. The weapon was generally deemed too heavy to hump during long search operations but was frequently flown in for assaults on fortified positions once contact was made.

A Blooper man from the 1st Infantry Division prepares to move into the assault during operations near the Saigon River in 1966.

With extra ammo at hand in his bunker position, a Republic of Korea (ROK)
soldier scans for targets over the sights of his M79 grenade launcher.

With his trusty Blooper at hand, a long-range patrol (LRRP)
soldier takes a break in heavy jungle cover.

An Army Specialist manning a position on the outskirts of
Saigon loads his M79 with a CS gas riot-control grenade.

A soldier set up with a supply of CS gas grenades and wearing a Field Protective
Mask prepares to fire a riot-control round on the outskirts of Saigon.

A trooper with the 173rd Airborne Brigade pushes forward
near Dak To with his M79 ready for instant action.

A soldier from the 1097th Transportation Company rides as convoy security armed with an M79 grenade launcher.

A pair of 4th Infantry Division Blooper men fire cover for fellow infantrymen moving into an assault near Duc Pho in 1967.

Armed with an M79, an M113 ACAV crewman keeps watch over dismounts sweeping a road during Operation Santa Fe.

A soldier from the 12th Infantry Regiment of the 4th Infantry Division keeps watch over a clearing on the outskirts of Saigon with his M79 at the ready.

An Australian Warrant Officer with a MACV advisory team teaches an ARVN trooper how to aim and fire the M79.

A grenadier with the 1st Air Cavalry Division slings his Blooper
prior to moving out for operations near An Khe in 1966.

A 9th Infantry Division grenadier operating in the Mekong Delta
fires his Blooper on suspected enemy positions near Long An.

In action on the outskirts of Saigon during Tet 1968, an ARVN
grenadier bloops a round into a suspected enemy position.

An ARVN Blooper Man helps load a wounded enemy
soldier into a vehicle for evacuation.

An M79 grenadier with the 25th Infantry Division secures
his weapon after a very wet river crossing in 1968.

An M113 crewman with the 5th Infantry Division (Mechanized) adds firepower to his vehicle with an M79 grenade launcher.

A Marine operating south of Danang in 1969 uses his M79
to conduct reconnaissance by fire on a treeline.

A 1st Marine Division grenadier operating near An Hoa in 1968 takes
an enemy position under fire with his Blooper. Like all M79 grenadiers,
he is armed with an M1911A1 pistol as a back-up weapon.

VC is an abbreviation for Viet Cong, or Vietnamese Communists. The VC were mostly irregular soldiers, although there were large permanent formations from around 1962 onwards. The NVA, or North Vietnamese Army, were regular troops and came from the northern provinces of Vietnam, and were armed with Soviet-style weapons. They were introduced into the war in late 1965.

VC AND NVA SMALL ARMS

VC & NVA SMALL ARMS

Contrary to some popular impressions of simple peasant farmers armed with pitchforks and machetes, the VC/NVA main units were well-equipped with modern arms either from Soviet bloc or Chinese sources.

Early operations against primarily Viet Cong guerilla units in Vietnam revealed that enemy forces were armed with a wide variety of infantry weapons from an even wider variety of sources. Many of the rifles, pistols, and light machineguns used by the VC were captured from Japanese or French forces during earlier conflicts in the country. These included such familiar weapons as U.S. M1 and M2 carbines, Thompson submachine guns in several variants, and the French MAT-49 or Chinese version of the Soviet PPSh-41 sub-guns. Logistics for VC units firing such a disparate spread of ammo types in these odd-lot weapons was always a nightmare but things became more organized—and more troublesome for allied forces—later in the war as more and more conventional North Vietnamese Army units entered the fray with a fairly standardized variety of battlefield small arms, most of Soviet or Chinese design and manufacture. By the time of the Tet Offensive in 1968, the NVA and Main Force VC were almost entirely armed with modern Soviet or Chicom weapons, although the regional and local VC forces still carried weapons of mixed vintage.

Pistols were more of a status symbol among VC and NVA forces in Vietnam than an effective infantry sidearm. U.S. and allied forces did not often encounter them, but when they did, enemy semi-autos such as the Soviet/Chicom 7.62mm TT-33 Tokarev and the 9mm Makarov usually became prized war trophies. By around 1966, the most common enemy infantry weapon encountered in Vietnam was the Soviet 7.62mm AK-47 assault rifle or its Chinese clone, the Type 56. This was a select-fire weapon capable of delivering either semi- or full-auto fire from a 30-round magazine that was rightfully admired by allied forces for its rugged reliability and feared for its lethality in close combat. Nearly as common in enemy hands by the time major NVA units were regularly encountered in South Vietnam was the Soviet Simonov semi-automatic rifle (commonly called the SKS) firing the same ammo as the AK from a 10-round internal magazine.

Light machineguns provided supporting fire for maneuvering VC and NVA units as it did for allied infantrymen in Vietnam. The most prevalent models were the older DPM firing a 7.62x54mm rimmed cartridge from a pancake drum magazine mounted horizontally atop the weapon, and the more common Degtyarev RPD (Chinese Type 56 LMG) that fired standard AK ammo from a metallic, reusable belt either packed into a drum magazine or feeding from loose belts. The RPD was lightweight—just a little over 16 pounds empty—fitted with a sturdy bipod, and easily manned by only a single gunner who could fire at a rate of about 700 rounds per minute, delivering fairly accurate coverage out to about 800 meters. The RPK which appeared relatively late in the war was a section support machinegun that looked like an overgrown AK with a snail-type drum magazine, longer barrel, and bipod fitted near the muzzle. Combat performance was basically the same as the RPD, but the RPK was more robust and could fire from the drum magazine (75 rounds), an extended 40-round box, or any standard 30-round AK magazine.

If the NVA forces fighting in South Vietnam during the war could be said to employ a medium or general purpose machinegun, it was the Soviet designed Goryonov SG-34 or the later variant SGM in 7.62mm. This was a truly crew-served weapon (usually two or three men) and often found mounted on a diminutive wheeled carriage that brought its combat weight up to nearly 90 pounds. While the Goryonov could be—and often was—used in an anti-aircraft role against allied helicopter operations, its most commonly encountered use was in a strongpoint by VC or NVA forces defending fortified positions. The machinegun was accurate, reliable, and rugged with a 1,500 meter effective range and 500-700 round-per-minute rate of fire.

The NVA forces also fielded a counterpart to the U.S. M2 heavy machinegun in the DShK-38/46 firing a 12.7mm round out to an effective range of 1,000 meters. This is a brute of a weapon weighing nearly 300 pounds on a wheeled carriage that made it only slightly less cumbersome to move along primitive trails and up jungle-covered mountains. The wheeled carriage included a set of tripod legs that could be unfolded and used to make the gun more stable. The DShK-38—often simply referred to as *Dashika*—was originally designed as an anti-aircraft weapon and the NVA often used it from fixed high-ground positions against helicopters or low-flying fixed-wing aircraft. It fired from a 250-round linked belt at a rate of 500-600 rounds per minute.

While the NVA and VC forces did not field a dedicated grenade launcher during the war in Vietnam, they were very adept at using captured U.S. M79s. There are also reports of NVA forces using flamethrowers, but these are rare. The flame weapon occasionally encountered was the Soviet LPO-50 man-pack variety with combat performance similar to U.S. flamethrowers.

While Viet Cong and NVA forces employed relatively few pistols in the field, the most common weapon encountered was the Soviet-designed Tokarev in 7.62 x 25mm usually in the form of the Chinese copy known as the Type 51 pistol.

U.S. soldiers learn about the ubiquitous AK-47 at
the Bear Cat Ranger School in 1970.

A typical haul of weapons after a battle with NVA forces includes RPGs, an RPD light machinegun, SKS carbines and many variations of the AK-47 assault rifle.

A wide variety of AK-47 variants were encountered in Vietnam during the war years. Pictured here are a Polish model, an AKM, and a folding stock AK-47.

A U.S. Marine from the 3rd Marine Division poses with a captured AK-47 in late 1965.

A U.S. Marine operating near the DMZ examines a Polish model AK-47 with folding stock.

An NVA soldier attempts to keep his AK-47 dry using flotation devices during a river crossing.

NVA troopers armed with AK-47s and supported by a B-40 rocket launcher in background rush past dead ARVN soldiers somewhere in South Vietnam circa 1970.

This often-published and clearly posed photo of a Viet Cong trooper standing guard outside a tunnel provides an excellent look at one of the most common semi-auto rifles used by VC and NVA forces, the Chinese Type 56 in 7.62 x 39mm. The rifle is an exact copy of the Soviet Simonov (SKS) and featured a folding bayonet with either a standard blade as depicted here or a spike blade depending on age and variant.

Another good look at a Chines Type 56 rifle captured by U.S. forces in 1967. This weapon has the spike-type folding bayonet.

BOLT-ACTION RIFLES

A wide variety of AK-47 variants were encountered in Vietnam during the war years. Pictured here are a Polish model, an AKM, and a folding stock AK-47.

Army intelligence specialists from the 173rd Airborne Brigade inventory a large cache of enemy weapons in late 1965. The variety is staggering but the majority of the captured rifles are typical bolt-action Moson-Nagant Model 1944s; some still in the padded wrapping that protected them on the trip down the Ho Chi Minh Trail.

Korean Marines take an enemy prisoner in southern I Corps during an operation in late 1967. The NVA being pulled from his fighting position has surrendered his Moson-Nagant bolt-action rifle.

This French MAS-36 bolt-action rifle was captured from a VC unit in early 1967. As the war ground on, fewer and fewer of these reliable old weapons, mostly captured during the earlier Indochina conflict with French colonial forces, were found by Americans on the battlefield.

Captured VC weapons taken during an operation near Saigon in 1967, some of which bear paperwork which will turn them into legal war souvenirs for the soldiers who made the capture. Bolt-action rifles were among the very few war trophies that could be claimed and brought home by Americans.

This relatively large cache of enemy weapons likely represents the firepower of a VC company. The take includes several light and general purpose medium machineguns as well as a wide variety of bolt-action rifles, some of which appear to be of crude local manufacture.

There is some serious battle damage to these captured weapons taken after a firefight in 1966. The rocket launcher is an RPG-2, commonly called a B-40 by Americans. The rifle at the bottom of the picture is a bog-standard Moson-Nagant Model 1944 with folding spike bayonet.

A pair of captured 20mm anti-aircraft weapons taken in the Mekong Delta area during 1967 is flanked by a typical spectrum of bolt-action weapons, including Mauser K98s and Moson-Nagants, likely carried by the infantrymen who served and protected the guns.

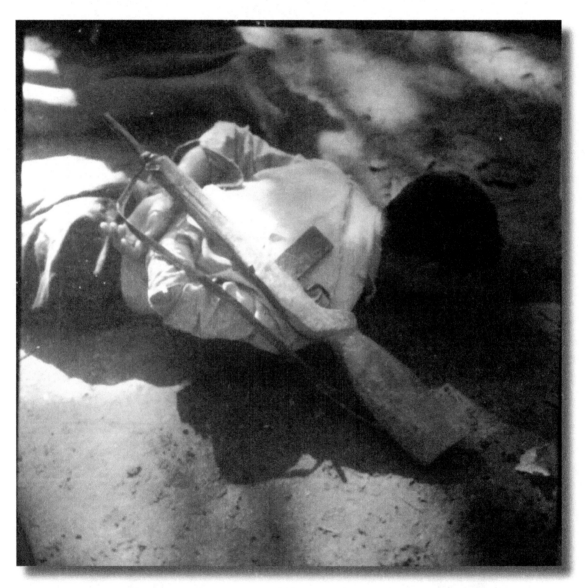

A rare look at an enemy training aid is provided in this photo of a Viet Cong guerrilla killed near an American base in 1966. The weapon is a non-firing mock-up of a U.S. M1 carbine that could be used to teach weapon handling or to intimidate villagers who didn't know the difference.

Viet Cong units employed a wide variety of elderly and modern weapons
in the war against South Vietnamese and allied forces including all
types of captured arms. This cache of weapons taken by a Mike Force
unit in 1969 includes U.S. M1 Garands, U.S. M1 and M2 carbines all
captured during encounters with ARVN regional or popular forces.
Also shown are a number of Chinese Type 56 (SKS) carbines.

These ARVN troopers have captured some unique weaponry from VC forces near Bien Hoa. Pictured are two weapons manufactured by local artisans including a skeletonized pistol that looks something like an illicit street-style zip-gun and an M1 carbine that has been modified into a short, bolt-action rifle.

Typical of VC resourcefulness in weapon manufacture or modification is the M16 at the bottom of the photo which has been modified into a carbine with the addition of a shortened barrel plus a forward hand guard and flash-suppressor from an M60 machinegun. The other weapons include a battle-damaged AK-47 and a U.S. M1 or M2 carbine that has been fitted with a pistol grip.

Shortly after being shot-down over North Vietnam, a U.S. Air Force B-52 crewman sits dejectedly on the wing of his crashed aircraft. Guarding him is an NVA trooper with either a Soviet or Chinese copy of the venerable PPSh-41 SMG.

French weapons such as this VC modified MAT-49 SMG were
encountered regularly during the early years of the war in Vietnam.
They gradually disappeared as the flood of Chinese and Soviet
weapons reached VC and NVA units fighting in South Vietnam.

Jungle workshops produced an amazing number of knock-off weapons such as this homemade SMG which has some features of the French MAT-49 and the Soviet PPSh-41, both familiar armaments to the Viet Cong.

Operating south of Danang in 1965, units of the 3rd Marine Division captured these weapons from local VC. This Marine is holding a pair of French MAT-49 SMGs while a Soviet-style Moisan-Nagant M44 carbine rests nearby on the sandbags.

South Vietnamese General Nguyn Cao Ky presents a captured K-50
SMG to Commandant of the Marine Corps General Wallace M.
Green who was on a battlefield visit in the early days of the war.

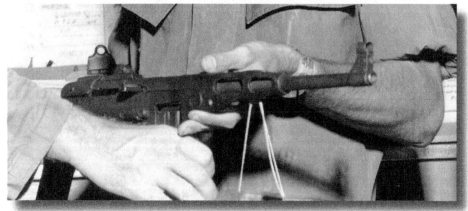

A close-up look at a captured Viet Cong K-50 SMG. The weapon is essentially
a copy of the Chinese Type 50 which was copied from the Soviet PPSh-41.

This photo showing a cache of enemy weapons captured near Danang during Tet 1968 provides an example of the wide variety of rifles, carbines, SMGs and light machineguns employed by VC and NVA units throughout the war.

This modified U.S. M1A1 Thompson SMG was captured by 1st Marine Division elements operating west of Danang in 1967. Thompsons captured from VC units typically were minus the butt-stock making the weapon less accurate but a bit easier to handle in thick jungle terrain.

Two more examples of jungle workshop efforts in Vietnam. At top is some sort of locally-manufactured weapon essentially based on the AK-47 action with all sorts of shady modifications. The weapon below is an almost exact copy of the British Sten made by VC artisans out of scrap metal.

LIGHT MACHINEGUNS

Female VC anti-air gun crew at watch behind a ZB-30 medium machinegun.
The weapon is a modification of the Czech ZB-26 firing 7.9mm ammo from
a 20-round magazine at the rate of around 600 rounds per minute.

An NVA gun crew preps a Goryonov SG-34 medium
machinegun for action while female porters move provisions
toward a unit training somewhere in North Vietnam.

One of the most common and effective infantry support weapons used by VC/NVA forces during the war was the Soviet RPD which fired the same 7.62 x 39mm cartridge as the bog standard AK-47.

This French M1924/29 light machinegun was an old but effective weapon in the hands of VC gun crews for much of the early years in Vietnam. It fired a 7.5mm cartridge from a 25-round box magazine feeding from the top of the weapon.

A good look at typical light machineguns captured by American forces. Most of these are Soviet or Chinese-supplied RPDs, the most common enemy LMG encountered on the battlefield.

A trooper with the Royal Australian Regiment displays a well-kept RPD captured by his unit on operations in 1968.

A soldier from the 9th Infantry Division sorts enemy weapons
captured near Bien Hoa in 1967. He is adding another Chinese
version of the DPM light machinegun to the pile.

A Viet Cong assault unit makes a water crossing with a BAR man in the bow. VC and NVA units made good use of any and all captured weapons although ammo resupply often presented a problem.

An NVA anti-air team practices with a version of the reliable and effective German MG-34.

A typical fire-support compliment for VC or NVA forces in
Vietnam included the RPG-2 and RPG-7 rocket launchers and
one or more of the RPD light machineguns shown here.

A treasure trove of enemy weapons seized by South Vietnamese Navy forces includes a DPM light machinegun and a variety of Chinese-manufactured PPSh-41s. On top of the pile at right is a relatively ancient PPD submachinegun loaded with a stick magazine vice the usual drum.

A small unit of Khmer Rouge irregulars mans a defensive position in Cambodia in 1970. The support weapon at center is a DPM light machinegun. Supporting that weapon are guerrillas armed with an American M16 and an SKS carbine with folding, blade-style bayonet. This is an example of the wide variety of weapons bought, sold, traded, used and re-used throughout the Southeast Asia arms bazaar.

HEAVY MACHINEGUNS

U.S. 9th Infantry Division soldiers display an American WW II vintage weapon captured from VC forces in the Mekong Delta. The weapon is the .30 caliber water-cooled version of the M1917 medium machinegun.

During Operation Dewey Canyon in the A Shau Valley in 1969, Marines collect heavy weapons captured from NVA forces. The Marine in foreground is carrying a DShK-38 heavy machinegun.

This photo of a U.S. solider examining a DShK-38 heavy machinegun provides a good look at the ring-style AA sight mounting and the ammo can from which the weapon is supplied with 12.7mm rounds.

The Goryonov SG-34 medium machinegun was a handy and reliable infantry support weapon among VC and NVA forces in Vietnam. The wheeled mount made it handy for dragging over round terrain.

In mid-1966 U.S. Marines began to encounter enemy forces equipped with heavy machineguns such as this DShK-38 that could do significant damage to their helicopters. This captured weapon is complete with tall tripod extensions and a small wheeled carriage to enhance mobility.

An American soldier takes a close look at an SG-34 medium machinegun that was captured complete with anti-air ring sight and wheeled carriage.

An interesting detailed look at a VC/NVA LPO flamethrower
rig captured in 1967. Fortunately for allied forces, encounters
with enemy flame weapons were relatively rare.

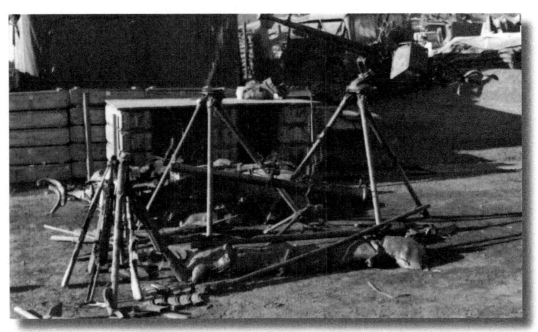

Featured in this photo of captured enemy weapons near Quang Tri in
1968 is a DShK-38 12.7mm heavy machinegun. This weapons, used
in both ground and anti-air configurations was the workhorse heavy
support weapon for NVA forces and a reliable helicopter killer.

This NVA rocket launcher rig captured by U.S. forces in 1969 shows the
complete system carried by an RPG gunner including carrying pouch, launcher
tube and rocket-propelled grenades with boosters and with tail-fins.

A Marine based at Dong Ha in 1967 shows off a captured RPG-7 launcher and projectile. The heavier, more-accurate RPG-7 replaced the RPG-2 (B-40) system and was seen more often in the field as the war progressed.

Viet Cong units were sometimes supplied with long-range high-explosive weapons like this 140mm rocket round captured unfired near Danang Air Base in 1968. These weapons were extremely inaccurate but did significant damage when rained down on close-packed personnel and equipment on many American installations. The device below the rocket is the point-detonating fuse which has been removed by EOD personnel.

Rocket rounds were often fired from crude or improvised launchers such as this one. The rockets were fired electrically; usually by simply hooking them up to a car or motorbike battery. When launchers were unavailable, the rockets could be simply placed on earthen ramps or berms built up to what the firing unit thought might be the necessary elevation to provide the required range to target.

This well-used RPG-2 system, commonly called the B-40 by American forces, shows the simple launch tube, a grenade and the booster cylinder. The B-40 was a simple weapon and very effective in combat despite a lack of long-range accuracy.

The U.S. 25th Infantry Division captured crates of B-40 rocket rounds during the 1970 incursion into Cambodia.

GRENADES

This photo of hand grenades employed by VC and NVA units in Vietnam shows the wide variety encountered by U.S. and allied forces. They ranged from very effective and lethal to pitch-and-pray models manufactured in jungle workshops.

While communist forces in Vietnam did not employ a grenade launcher equivalent to the U.S. M79, they were adept and effective at making and using many hand grenade variants, usually of the stick-handle type that were easy to arm and throw.

Typical Chinese-style stick-handle grenades captured fresh from delivery into South Vietnam in 1965.

VC and NVA units made good use of mortars in their field operations. They were equipped with Chinese 82mm medium tubes and 61mm light mortars such as these. Light mortars plus B-40s more than made up for their lack of an effective grenade launcher such as the U.S. M79.

Featured in this stash of captured enemy weapons is a Goryunov SG-43 medium machinegun on a wheeled carriage. It was a simple and effective weapon that could be used in infantry support or anti-air configurations with a ring-configured sight for leading allied helicopters or fixed-wing aircraft.

To supplement their field arsenal, VC units often used punji stakes, sometimes coated with human or animal excrement to wound allied soldiers patrolling in hostile territory. A penetrating wound from a punji stake, usually buried points-up in pits along trails or jungle paths, could cause infections and take the wounded soldier out of action.

Local Viet Cong units operating on a relative shoestring often employed native weapons such as this crossbow pictured with a flare pistol used for signalling in attacks on U.S. units.

AFTERWORD

BY TOM LAEMLEIN

From the end of World War II in 1945 through the fall of Saigon in 1975, the conflict in Southeast Asia brought together an incredible array of infantry weapons from around the world. Vietnam became an international arms bazaar of outrageous proportions, featuring weapons that dated from the late 19th Century to the most advanced contemporary small arms available to the global superpowers engaged in the rather heated cold war of the late 20th Century.

I am an image collector and researcher, and I've worked on multiple photo studies covering military firearms. Collecting images for this book was not only challenging, it was an amazing learning experience. Just when I thought I had a handle on the depth and breadth of the small arms used in Vietnam, a photo of something new, unique, and incredibly rare would crop up. That would spur me on to look for more, searching for that special image of a rare weapon or an unusual modification. Eventually, a researcher has to stop searching and start publishing. And that is how this book came to be.

I was honored when Dale Dye agreed to write the text to describe the images I had collected. He is one of America's finest military historians, and a highly qualified storyteller, particularly when it comes to the small arms used in Vietnam. After three tours of duty, 31 combat actions, and earning the Bronze Star (with Combat "V") as well as the Purple Heart, Captain Dye has either fired or been fired upon with almost every firearm deployed in Vietnam. He knows all too well about the weapons shown in these pages.

There is much to be learned by looking at these photographs. Each reader will take away something special, and their eye will capture unique details that I might be blind to. The sum total of the image collection gathered here represents an intimate look at the essential tools of a long and brutal infantryman's war. It is my hope that this book helps us grow in our respect and admiration for our veteran's sacrifices—and help us learn to cherish the peace.

I would like to thank Mike Morton of Springfield, Missouri and Jim Wagner of Rochester, New York for their help and contributions.

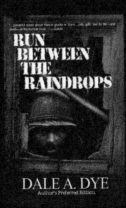
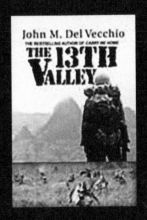

CPSIA information can be obtained
at www.ICGtesting.com
Printed in the USA
LVOW05s2209300118
564504LV00049B/423/P